CONTENTS

Angels We Have Heard on High	5
Away in a Manger	27
Hark! the Herald Angels Sing	23
Infant Holy, Infant Lowly	34
It Came Upon the Midnight Clear	20
Joy to the World	36
O Come, All Ye Faithful	2
Silent Night! Holy Night!	11
We Three Kings	30
What Child Is This?	15

lillenas | PO Box 419527
PUBLISHING COMPANY | Kansas City, MO 64141
a division of nazarene publishing house

O Come, All Ye Faithful

Fanfare

JOHN FRANCIS WADE
Arranged by Phillip Keveren

Song ending

a tempo

Optional transition ending

a tempo

rit.

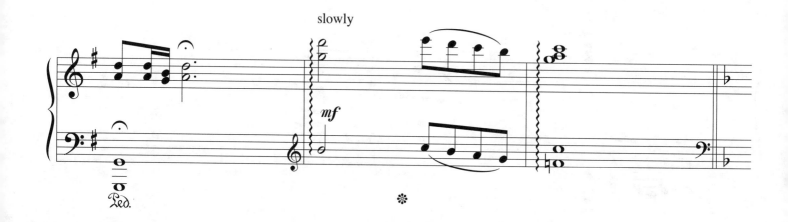

slowly

mf

Ped.

Angels We Have Heard on High

Traditional French Melody
Arranged by Phillip Keveren

Flowing, with expression ♩ = ca. 150

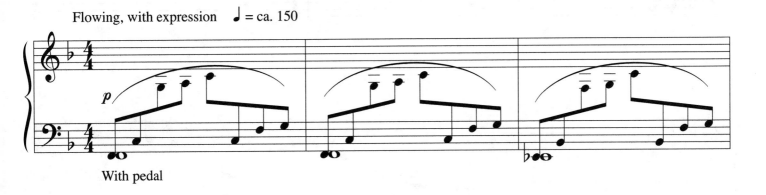

With pedal

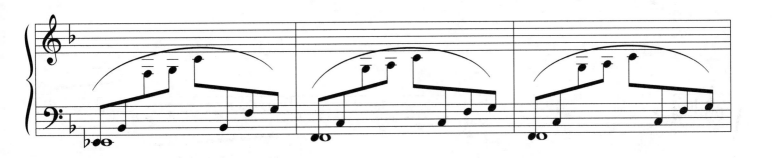

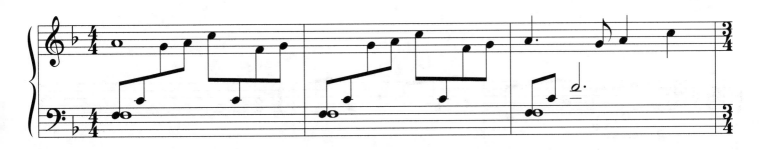

Silent Night! Holy Night!

FRANZ GRUBER
Arranged by Phillip Keveren

Song ending

molto rit.

Optional transition ending

What Child Is This?

Traditional English Melody
Arranged by Phillip Keveren

It Came upon the Midnight Clear

RICHARD S. WILLIS
Arranged by Phillip Keveren

Peacefully ♩. = ca. 40

Hark! the Herald Angels Sing

FELIX MENDELSSOHN
Arranged by Phillip Keveren

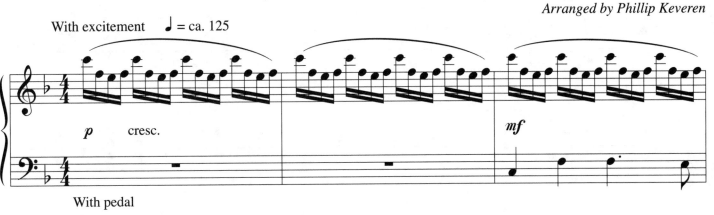

Away in a Manger

JAMES R. MURRAY
Arranged by Phillip Keveren

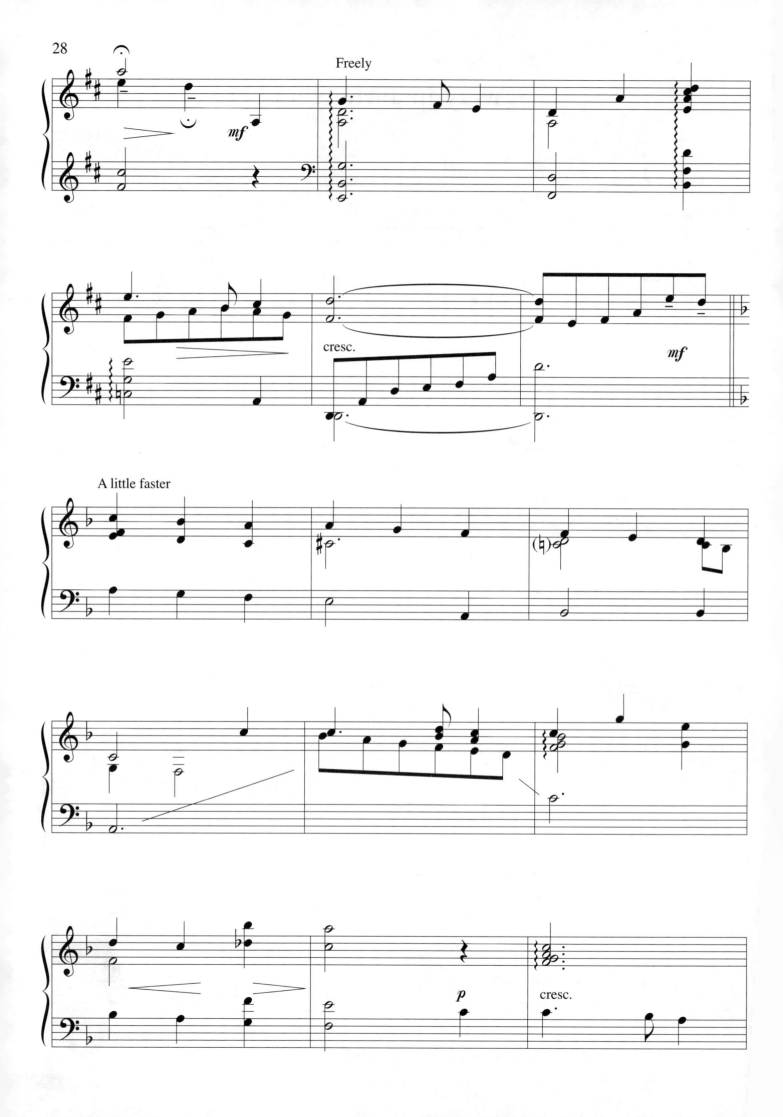

We Three Kings

JOHN H. HOPKINS, JR.
Arranged by Phillip Keveren

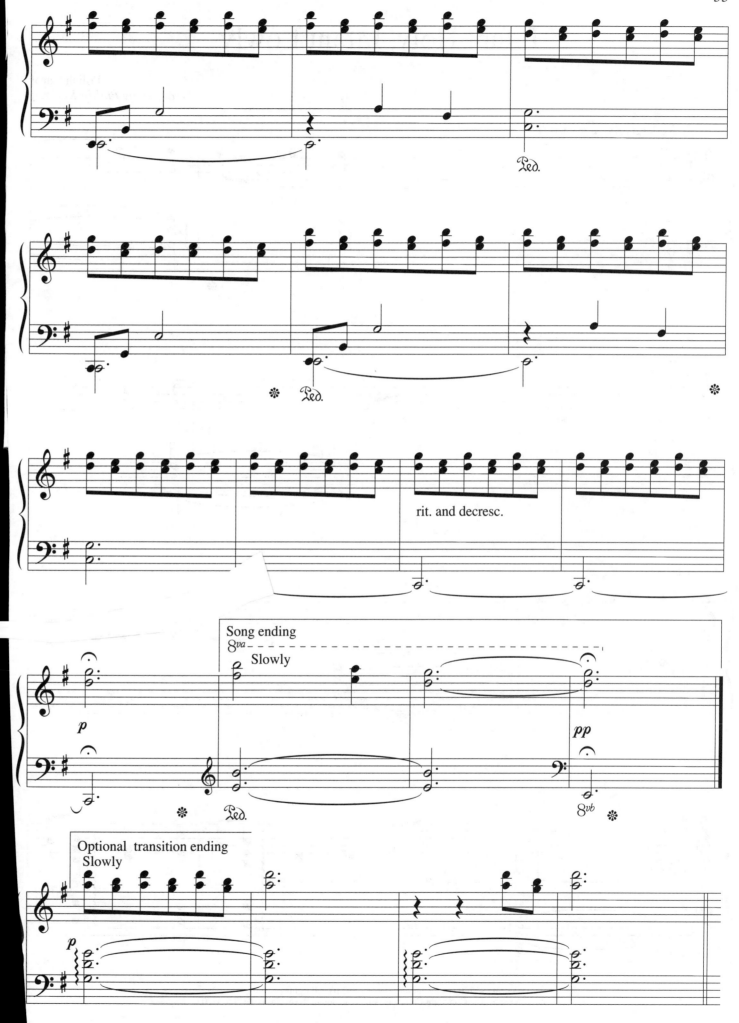

Infant Holy, Infant Lowly

Polish Carol
Arranged by Phillip Keveren

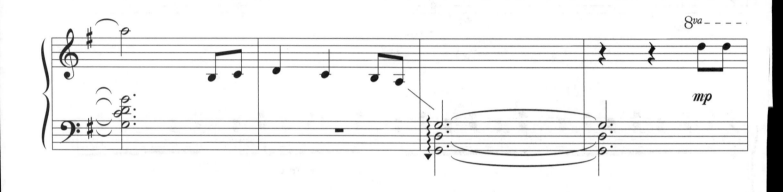

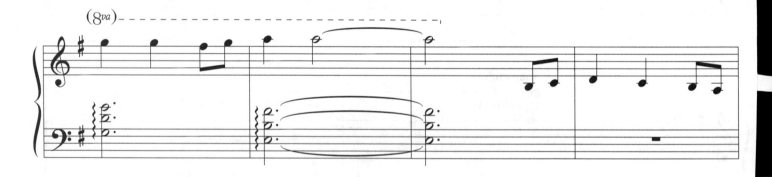

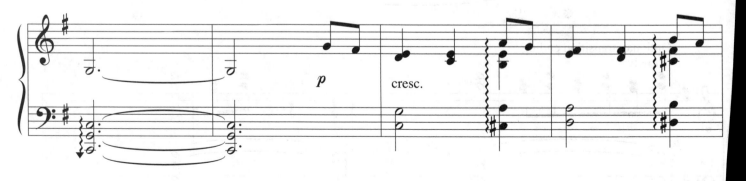

Joy to the World

GEORGE FREDERICK HANDEL
Arranged by Phillip Keveren

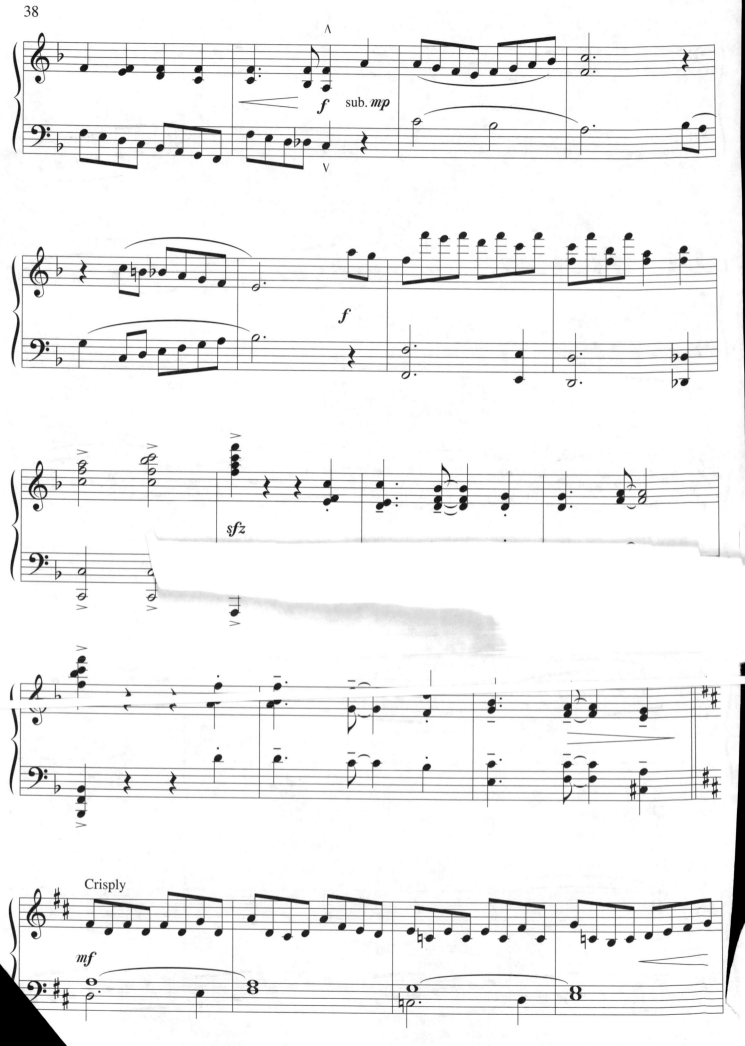